# ENVIRONMENTAL FOOTPRINTS

## How Big Is Your Travel Footprint?

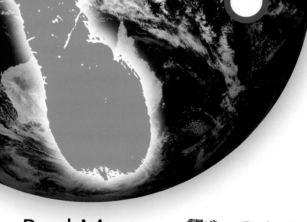

Paul Mason

 **Marshall Cavendish**
Benchmark

New York

This edition first published in 2010 in the United States of America by Marshall Cavendish Benchmark.

Marshall Cavendish Benchmark
99 White Plains Road
Tarrytown, NY 10591
www.marshallcavendish.us

First published in 2008 by
MACMILLAN EDUCATION AUSTRALIA PTY LTD
15–19 Claremont Street, South Yarra 3141

Visit our website at www.macmillan.com.au or go directly to www.macmillanlibrary.com.au

Associated companies and representatives throughout the world.

Copyright © Paul Mason 2008

Library of Congress Cataloging-in-Publication Data

Mason, Paul.
  How big is your travel footprint? / by Paul Mason.
  p. cm. – (Environmental footprints)
  Includes index.
  ISBN 978-0-7614-4415-2
  1. Travel–Environmental aspects–Juvenile literature. 2. Transportation–Environmental aspects–Juvenile literature. 3. Travel–Environmental aspects–Case studies–Juvenile literature. 4. Transportation–Environmental aspects–Case studies–Juvenile literature.  I. Title.
  G156.5.E58M37 2009
  910.4–dc22

                                                        2008048104

Edited by Anna Fern
Text and cover design by Cristina Neri, Canary Graphic Design
Page layout by Domenic Lauricella
Photo research by Legend Images
Illustrations by Nives Porcellato and Andrew Craig

Printed in the United States

**Acknowledgments**
The author and the publisher are grateful to the following for permission to reproduce copyright material:

Front cover photograph: Earth from space © Jan Rysavy/iStockphoto; colored footprint © Rich Harris/iStockphoto. Images repeated throughout title.

Photos courtesy of:
AAP/AP Photo/Jonny Mattsson, **11**; © Cdromey/Dreamstime.com, **30**; © Vansciver/Dreamstime.com, **14**; Hamish Blair/ALLSPORT/Getty Images, **25**; David Hecker/AFP/Getty Images, **13**; Mark Ralston/AFP/Getty Images, **23**; © Ramon Berk/iStockphoto, **7**; © Grant Dougall/iStockphoto, **18**; © eddl/iStockphoto, **26**; © Fleyeing/iStockphoto, **21**; © Richard Foreman/iStockphoto, **16**; © Ian Jeffery/iStockphoto, **12**; © Brandon Laufenberg/iStockphoto, **3** (top right), **6**; © mandygodbehear/iStockphoto, **10**; © Vasko Miokovic/iStockphoto, **8**; © malcolm romain/iStockphoto, **28**; © Wouter van Caspel/iStockphoto, **22**; © Vasiliki Varvaki/iStockphoto, **27**; Photos.com, **29**; © Marcus Brown/Shutterstock, **20**; © egd/Shutterstock, **15**; © Anton Foltin/Shutterstock, **24**; © Brian Tan/Shutterstock, **5**; Wikipedia Public Domain, **19**.

While every care has been taken to trace and acknowledge copyright, the publisher tenders their apologies for any accidental infringement where copyright has proved untraceable. Where the attempt has been unsuccessful, the publisher welcomes information that would redress the situation.

**Please note**
At the time of printing, the Internet addresses appearing in this book were correct. Owing to the dynamic nature of the Internet, however, we cannot guarantee that all these addresses will remain correct.

0972
1 3 5 6 4 2

# Contents

Environmental Footprints    4

The Transportation Industry    6

Building Vehicles    10

*Case Study* Wolfsburg Volkswagen Factory    13

Pollution from Travel    14

*Case Study* Cyclocity    19

Traffic Congestion    20

*Case Study* Dongtan, the World's First Eco-city    23

Transportation Systems    24

*Case Study* The Walking Bus    27

How Big Is Your Travel Footprint?    28

Future Travel Footprints    30

Glossary    31

Index    32

## Glossary Words

When a word is printed in **bold**, you can look up its meaning in the Glossary on page 31.

# Environmental Footprints

This book is about the footprints people leave behind them. But these are special footprints. They are the footprints people leave on the **environment**.

## Heavy Footprints

Some people leave heavy, long-lasting footprints. They do this by:

- acting in ways that harm the environment
- using up lots of **natural resources**, including water, land, and energy

It can be hundreds of years before the environment recovers from heavy footprints.

## Light Footprints

Other people leave light, short-lived footprints. They do this by:

- behaving in ways that harm the environment as little as possible
- using the smallest amount of natural resources they can.

The environment recovers from light footprints much more quickly.

As the world's population grows, more natural resources will be needed. It will be important not to waste resources if we are to leave light footprints.

The world's population is expected to continue growing in the future.

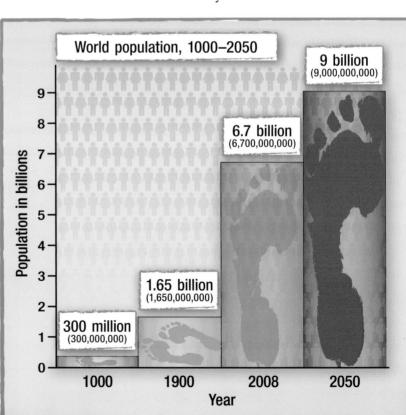

World population, 1000–2050

9 billion (9,000,000,000)

6.7 billion (6,700,000,000)

1.65 billion (1,650,000,000)

300 million (300,000,000)

Population in billions

Year

# What Makes Up a Travel Footprint?

A travel footprint is made up of the effects on the environment of the journeys people make. Travel footprints are made by:

⊕ the resources used to make **vehicles** in which people travel

⊕ the **pollution** caused by the fuel that powers vehicles

⊕ the environmental effects of building roads, railroads, train stations, and airports

All these things have an effect on the environment. The bigger the effect, the heavier the footprint left behind.

The choices people make about how they travel can have a big effect on the environment.

What sort of travel footsteps are you taking? Read on to find out!

# The Transportation Industry

The transportation industry is made up of everything needed for people to travel from place to place. It includes making vehicles, fuel for vehicles, and building routes for vehicles to travel on.

## Today's Transportation System

Today, the **transportation system** is an important part of most people's lives. It gets them to school and work, brings them food, and takes them on vacation. People use many different types of transportation, and each one has a different travel footprint.

### Human-Powered Travel

Human-powered travel includes walking, cycling, and skateboarding. Human-powered travel is fueled by the traveler's own energy, such as when riding a bicycle, and causes no pollution. This means human-powered travel has a light footprint.

Cycling is an environmentally friendly way to travel.

## Cars, Motorbikes, and Scooters

Cars, motorbikes, and scooters only carry a small number of passengers. The vehicles have to be refilled with fuel to keep going. The resources used to build them and the fuel they use mean these vehicles have a heavier footprint than human-powered travel.

## Airplanes, Buses, and Trains

Building big vehicles such as airplanes, buses, and trains uses lots of resources. If these vehicles are built to last a long time, they will have a lighter footprint. Big vehicles, however, do use a lot of fuel, which adds to their footprint.

Airplanes use a lot of fuel and resources, so air travel leaves a heavy footprint.

### Rethink!

For a lighter footprint, make journeys of less than 2 miles (3.2 kilometers) by walking or cycling.

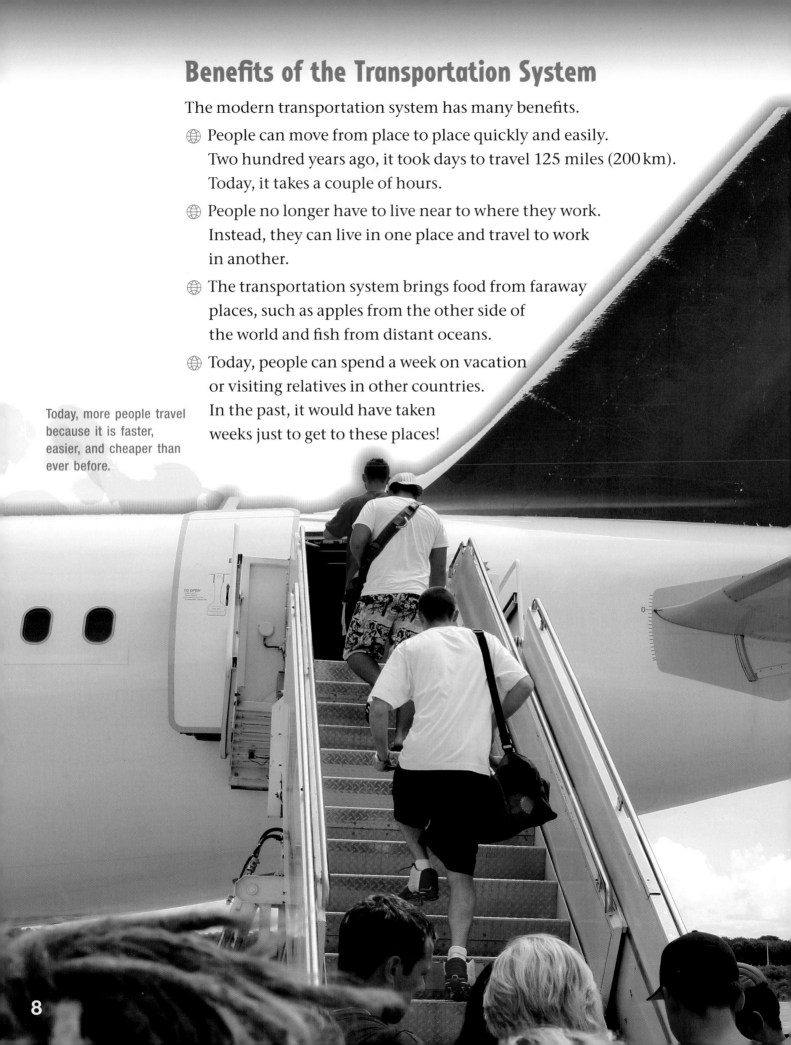

# Benefits of the Transportation System

The modern transportation system has many benefits.

- 🌐 People can move from place to place quickly and easily. Two hundred years ago, it took days to travel 125 miles (200 km). Today, it takes a couple of hours.

- 🌐 People no longer have to live near to where they work. Instead, they can live in one place and travel to work in another.

- 🌐 The transportation system brings food from faraway places, such as apples from the other side of the world and fish from distant oceans.

- 🌐 Today, people can spend a week on vacation or visiting relatives in other countries. In the past, it would have taken weeks just to get to these places!

Today, more people travel because it is faster, easier, and cheaper than ever before.

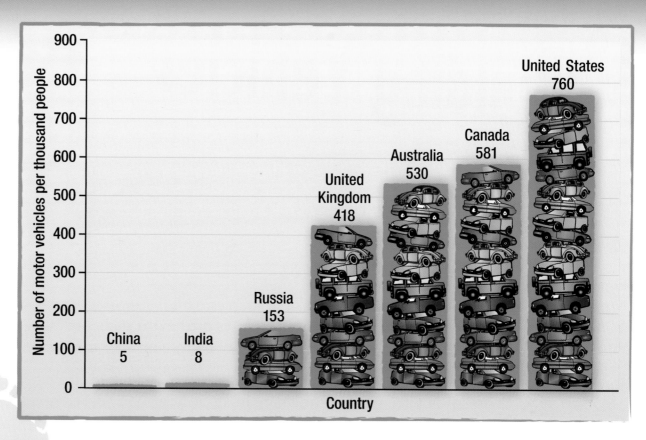

*Number of motor vehicles per thousand people*

| Country | Value |
|---------|-------|
| China | 5 |
| India | 8 |
| Russia | 153 |
| United Kingdom | 418 |
| Australia | 530 |
| Canada | 581 |
| United States | 760 |

Vehicle ownership is increasing rapidly in some countries. In China, for example, it is predicted that by 2010 there will be forty cars for every 1,000 people.

# Environmental Costs of the Transportation System

The transportation system affects the world's environment in many ways.

- Making vehicles uses up precious resources, such as energy, water, metals, and chemicals.
- The fuels that are used to run many vehicles, especially **fossil fuels**, create harmful pollution.
- The increasing number of vehicles causes roads to become clogged up, or congested.
- Building roads, railroads, and airports uses up precious resources and land. The developments cover over land that has been home to plants and animals.
- Vehicles that no longer work are thrown away. This adds to a mountain of waste that hangs around for thousands of years, polluting the environment.

All these things come at a cost to the environment, and make travel footprints heavier.

# Building Vehicles

The vehicles people travel in, from bicycles to airplanes, use up resources when they are built. Vehicles that use the least resources and last the longest have the lightest footprints.

## Using Up Resources

Making new vehicles uses up resources. This is part of their travel footprint. Many parts of cars, such as the fabrics used in car seats, are made from petroleum oil. The world's supplies of petroleum are running out.

Many other resources are used to make new vehicles. Even a bicycle contains metal, rubber, plastic, and foam. Imagine how many different resources are used to build a new airplane!

Making these bikes used metal, rubber, plastic, and other materials.

### Rethink!

As a way of saving resources, try fixing up an old bike instead of getting a new one.

Lots of energy is used when making new vehicles.

## Waste in Vehicle Factories

The factories where vehicles are made create a lot of waste. In some countries, strict rules prevent this waste from being released into the environment. In other countries, especially poorer countries, the rules are not as strict. The waste is released into the environment, causing pollution.

## Energy Use in Vehicle Factories

Making vehicles uses up a lot of energy. This energy is produced mainly by burning fossil fuels. Burning fossil fuels causes pollution. Pollution from burning fossil fuels is slowly changing Earth's climate, making it warmer. This is harming the environment all around the world.

## Longer-Lasting Vehicles

One way to make a vehicle's footprint lighter is to make the vehicle so that it lasts longer. Doing this makes the most of the resources that went into its manufacture. Making a vehicle that lasts twenty years is likely to use up fewer resources than making two vehicles that each last ten years.

## Recyclable Vehicles

Recyclable vehicles are vehicles of which many of the parts can be used again. For example, the metal parts of a car can be melted down and the metal used again. Recycling old metal in this way means that new **metal ore** does not have to be **mined**.

You will haver a lighter travel footprint if you drive a small, lightweight car instead of a heavy camper like this one.

Choosing to travel in vehicles that have been manufactured without waste and designed to last will give you a lighter travel footprint.

# Case Study
## Wolfsburg Volkswagen Factory

Many car **manufacturers** are trying to make their environmental footprints lighter. One of these is Volkswagen. Volkswagen's modern factory in Wolfsburg, Germany, has many light-footprint features.

🌐 All the **packaging** from deliveries to the factory is sorted and recycled. In 2006, this was more than 1,100 tons (1,000 metric tons) of packaging.

🌐 The factory keeps a store of reusable parts from old vehicles, which can be used instead of manufacturing new ones.

🌐 A waste center sorts all the factory's waste products ready for recycling.

🌐 The factory recycles water so that it uses the smallest possible amount of drinking water in its industrial processes.

Visitors can take a "green tour" and see how the factory tries to make its environmental footprint as light as possible.

These shiny new Volkswagens are ready to leave the light-footprint Wolfsburg factory to be sold.

# Pollution from Travel

Many vehicles are powered by burning fossil fuels, which causes pollution. There are, however, alternatives for people who want to have a lighter travel footprint.

## Fossil Fuels and Global Warming

Burning fossil fuels to power vehicles harms the environment. It releases polluting **greenhouse gases** into Earth's **atmosphere**. These gases trap heat, and slowly cause Earth's temperature to rise. This slow rise in temperature is called **global warming**.

Many scientists say that global warming is seriously damaging the environment. Sea levels are rising, threatening to flood low-lying coastal areas. Land that once grew crops is becoming **desert**. The weather is becoming more extreme, with more **hurricanes**, **droughts**, cold winters, and hot summers.

Exhaust gases from cars and trucks pollute the air.

Journeys in vehicles that are not full cause heavy travel footprints.

## Pollution per Person

Some ways of traveling cause more pollution per person, and a heavier travel footprint, than others.

⊕ One car might release 8 ounces (227 grams) of pollution every mile.

If the car is carrying one person, that person is causing 8 ounces of pollution for every mile they travel.

⊕ One bus might release 34 ounces (964 grams).

If the bus has 60 people on board, each person is causing only 0.57 ounces (16 grams) of pollution per mile. That's fourteen times less pollution than one person in a car.

*Rethink!*

Sharing a ride with other people instead of going in separate vehicles causes less pollution.

# Less Polluting Ways to Travel

There are ways to reduce the amount of pollution caused by our everyday travel.

### Hybrid Cars

Hybrid cars use more than one type of fuel. The most common type of hybrid car uses a combination of fossil fuel and electricity. When the car is running using electricity, it does not release any pollution, so its footprint becomes lighter.

Some people argue that hybrid cars are not much better than ordinary fossil-fuel cars, because their electricity often comes from power stations that burn fossil fuels.

This hybrid car is fueled by both gasoline and electricity.

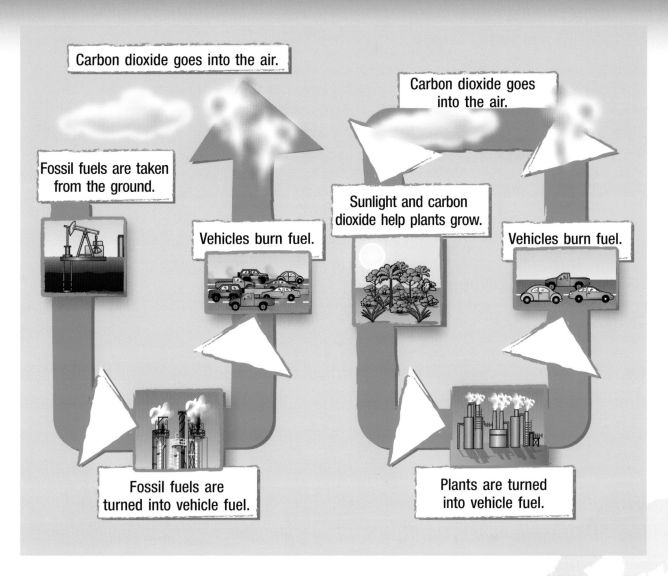

Carbon dioxide, one of the causes of global warming, is released by burning fossil fuels. Plants take carbon dioxide out of the air to help them grow, so using fuel made from plants is more environmentally friendly.

## Alternative Fuels

Alternative fuels are non-fossil fuels. The two main alternative fuels are **biodiesel** and **ethanol**. Both of these fuels are produced from plants. When the plants for these fuels are growing, they take in harmful **carbon dioxide** from the atmosphere. When they are burned as fuel, they release the carbon dioxide back into the atmosphere.

When fossil fuels are burned, they release an extra load of carbon dioxide that has not been in the atmosphere for millions of years. Overall, burning biodiesel and ethanol releases far fewer greenhouse gases than fossil fuels.

## Multiple-Occupancy Lanes

Multiple-occupancy lanes, or carpool lanes, can be used only by cars carrying more than one person. Multiple-occupancy lanes encourage people to travel together because traffic in these lanes moves quickly. Three people traveling together in one car makes less pollution than three people traveling in their own cars.

## Public Transportation

Public transportation is transportation that anyone can use, such as trains, buses, and streetcars. A bus carrying sixty people causes very little pollution per person. Using public transportation instead of a car makes people's footprints lighter.

## Cycling Networks

Many cities and towns now have networks of safe cycling routes. Cyclists travel safely along special lanes in the road, whizzing past the traffic and producing no pollution.

These bicycle commuters in Denmark produce no pollution and often get where they are going more quickly than cars!

Choosing to travel in ways that minimize pollution from burning fossil fuels will give you a lighter environmental footprint.

# Case Study
## Cyclocity

Cyclocity is a scheme that aims to make it easy to travel around cities by bike, without even owning a bicycle! Cyclocity has been successfully introduced in a number of European cities.

Bikes in the Cyclocity scheme are parked in special spots around the city. People swipe their membership card before borrowing a bike. Once they have finished their journey, the bike can be returned to any of the special parking spots. They swipe their card again and are charged a small fee for borrowing the bike.

Bikes in the scheme are fitted with electronic tags so that they cannot be stolen.

Every journey made by bike instead of by car reduces the cyclist's travel footprint.

Shared city bicycles can be found in special parking spots around many cities, ready for commuters to use.

# Traffic Congestion

As the world's population gets bigger and richer, more people will be able to afford cars and other vehicles. The roads could start to become increasingly busy, or congested.

## Congestion and the Environment

Traffic congestion harms the environment. Cars stopped in congestion usually still have their engines running. They are still burning fossil fuels and causing pollution. The people in the cars are making their travel footprint heavier, without actually moving!

Many people in poorer countries travel by bicycle, bus, or train, and have only light travel footprints, compared to people who travel by car.

## Increasing Congestion

When roads become congested, the traffic moves very slowly, or sometimes stops completely. Congestion is an increasing problem, especially in cities. Around the world, many city governments are trying to find ways of stopping congestion. In London, in the United Kingdom, drivers who go into the city center are charged a fee as a way of discouraging unnecessary journeys.

## Increasing Population

Most experts think that the world's population will increase to 9 billion (9,000,000,000) by 2050. The population is currently 6 billion. If all these extra people travel in the same way as today, congestion will increase considerably.

A long traffic jam comes to a standstill on a highway in Belgium.

# Ways to Reduce Congestion

There are ways to reduce the amount of congestion caused by our everyday travel.

## Public Transportation

Trains, buses, and streetcars are the most common types of public transportation. These can carry large numbers of people and, because they take up less space on the roads, they cause less congestion than cars.

## Cycle Networks

The big networks of special routes for cyclists in many large cities make it easier and safer to travel by bicycle. Bicycles take up hardly any space on the road, so they cause very little congestion.

## Mixed Developments

Mixed developments are areas where homes, schools, workplaces, and stores are close together. They make it easier for people to avoid traveling in ways that cause congestion. Instead of driving, people are able to walk from place to place. They spend less time traveling, and have lighter travel footprints too!

These people are riding in a cycle lane on the sidewalk in Berlin, Germany.

Choosing to travel in ways that minimize congestion will give you a lighter travel footprint.

# Case Study

## Dongtan, the World's First Eco-city

The Chinese Government is planning to build the world's first eco-city. The city will produce no environment-harming pollution. It will have a number of special features.

- Gasoline and diesel vehicles will be banned.
- Workplaces and homes will be built side by side.
- Public transportation will carry people from place to place.

- The city's energy will come from non-fossil fuels.
- Buildings will be insulated to make sure they keep in the heat, and do not waste energy.

The city, named Dongtan, will be home to 500,000 people. It is to be built on an island near Shanghai.

This wetland bird sanctuary will surround Dongtan when the city is built in 2010.

# Transportation Systems

Transportation systems are made up of roads, railroads, airports, and other modes of transport. Building these harms the environment in several ways, adding to the travel footprints of people who use them.

## Building Transportation Systems

Building and maintaining transportation systems uses up resources. Every new road uses up metal, rock, and other raw materials that cannot be replaced.

Building roads and parking lots covers the earth with hard, waterproof material. Water runs off into drains instead of soaking into the soil. As a result, the surrounding area does not get as much water. This can make it difficult for trees, plants, and animals to survive.

Building new roads uses up lots of resources and leaves a heavy footprint.

Airplanes release their pollution high up in the sky, where it does more harm than pollution that is released lower down.

## Impacts of New Roads

Increasing traffic has led to new roads being built. New roads cut through the habitats of animals and plants. With people and traffic there is also increased litter and noise. New roads also make it possible for industries such as logging and mining to move into new areas and destroy previously undisturbed habitat.

## Air Travel and Airports

Air travel makes people's travel footprints much heavier. Airplanes cause more pollution for each mile traveled than any other form of transportation.

Building new airports means that more air traffic can come and go, causing more harm to the environment.

### Rethink!

People who travel by plane can reduce their footprints by paying for trees to be planted. The trees take in the pollution that the plane releases.

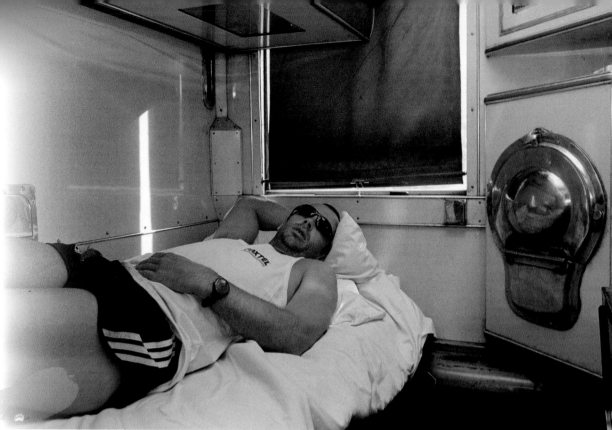

Traveling long distances overnight on a train is a good way to avoid air travel.

# Reducing Vehicles on the Road

Reducing vehicle numbers makes it unnecessary to build new roads. There are several things people can do so that there are fewer cars on the road.

- Make short journeys of less than 2 miles (3.2 km) on foot or bicycle.
- Use buses and trains if you cannot walk or cycle. They can be used instead of a car for long journeys.
- Share car rides with others who regularly travel to the same place. That way, there are fewer cars on the road.

# Avoiding Air Travel

If fewer people travel by air, there will be less need for more airports to be built. Today, many people are choosing to make their footprint smaller by traveling on vacation using public transportation instead of airplanes.

Reducing the number of journeys you take by car and by airplane gives you a lighter travel footprint.

# Case Study
## The Walking Bus

Instead of driving young children to school, people can reduce their travel footprint by using a walking bus.

A walking bus is made up of a group of children who walk to school together. They follow the same route every day.

Parents walk their children to the route, where they join the walking bus as it passes. Two adults walk with the bus, one at the front and one at the back. They make sure the children are safe. Walking buses make thousands of car rides a year unnecessary.

Walking to school is great exercise and does no harm to the environment.

# How Big Is Your Travel Footprint?

The size of a person's travel footprint depends on the kind of vehicle they use, and how often and how far they travel. How big do you think your footprint is?

## What Kind of Vehicle Do You Use?

Vehicles with a light environmental footprint:

- do not use lots of resources when they are manufactured
- last a long time
- are made of recyclable material
- use little or no fossil fuel per person
- use less-polluting, **renewable** fuel such as biodiesel

How big do you think your travel footprint is?

Walking does no harm to the environment, so traveling on foot has a light environmental footprint.

# What Kind of Journeys Do You Make?

People with a light travel footprint travel short distances on foot, by bicycle, or public transportation. For longer journeys, they travel by public transportation instead of by car or airplane.

# Work Out Your Travel Footprint!

Record the number of journeys you make every day for a week. The results might look like this:

| | |
|---|---|
| Walking | 10 |
| Cycling | 4 |
| Car | 14 |
| Public transportation | 4 |
| TOTAL JOURNEYS | 32 |

Turn these numbers into percentages. If 10 of your total 32 journeys were made walking:

$10 \div 32 \times 100 = 31$ percent.

That means that 31 percent or about one-third of your journeys have almost no travel footprint.

In London, United Kingdom, most vehicles have to pay to go into the center of the city, but light-footprint vehicles such as bicycles and scooters can travel free.

congestion charging zone

C

Mon - Fri
7 am - 6 pm

1 mile ahead

Except buses

C.London
Euston
A400

Making a big percentage of journeys by walking, cycling, or public transportation means you have a light travel footprint.

# Future Travel Footprints

You can choose to take light footsteps or heavy footsteps. If people continue leaving heavy footprints, it could affect the environment for thousands of years to come.

## What You Can Do

The Internet is a great way to find out more about what you can do to take lighter footsteps. Try visiting these websites:

⊕ **http://www.epa.gov/greenvehicles/**
This site lets you compare how much pollution comes from different models of cars and other vehicles.

⊕ **http://www.greencycling.blogspot.com/**
This is the blog of a pair of young women who decided to cycle across North America. Their trip raised money for an environmental campaigning organization.

Some of the search terms you might use to find interesting information about travel and the environment include:

⊕ walking bus
⊕ greenhouse gas
⊕ cycling
⊕ human-powered vehicles
⊕ environmental costs of flying.

Repairing an old bike instead of buying a new one will help lighten your travel footprint.

What will YOU do to change your travel footprint in the future?

# Glossary

**atmosphere**
the layer of gases that surrounds Earth, enabling humans, animals, plants, and other creatures to survive

**biodiesel**
fuel made from the oil of plants such as peanuts, which does not cause pollution

**carbon dioxide**
a gas that is used by plants to help them grow, and which is released when fossil fuels are burned

**desert**
area with very little water, where only certain plants and animals can live

**droughts**
periods of time without enough rainfall, when water becomes scarce, crops fail, and plants and animals suffer or die

**environment**
the natural world, including plants, animals, land, rivers, and seas

**ethanol**
a type of fuel made from plants such as wheat

**fossil fuels**
the remains of plants and animals from millions of years ago, which have been buried deep under Earth's surface and there turned into coal, oil, and gas

**global warming**
process by which Earth's average temperature is getting warmer

**greenhouse gases**
gases that are contributing to global warming, many of which are released when fossil fuels are burned

**hurricanes**
violent storms with very high winds, capable of damaging buildings, trees, and other things

**manufacturers**
factories that make raw materials into products for people to buy and use

**metal ore**
rock from which metal can be extracted

**mined**
dug out of the ground

**natural resources**
natural substances, such as wood, metal, coal, or water, which can be used by humans

**packaging**
the wrapping for the things people buy, such as cardboard boxes, plastic bags, cans, and foam cartons

**pollution**
damaging substances, especially chemicals or waste products, that harm the environment

**renewable**
capable of being easily replaced

**transportation system**
network of roads, railroads, airports, canals, and shipping routes that allows goods and people to be transported around

**vehicles**
devices for carrying people or goods from place to place

# Index

**A**

air travel,   7, 25, 26
alternative fuels,   17

**B**

biodiesel,   17, 28
building roads,   9, 24–25
buses,   7, 15, 18, 26

**C**

carbon dioxide,   17
carpool,   18, 26
cars,   7, 9, 15, 16, 20–1
cycling,   6, 7, 18, 19, 20-21, 22,
    26, 30
Cyclocity scheme,   19

**D**

developing countries,   9, 11
Dongtan, China,   23

**E**

eco-cities,   23
electricity,   16
energy,   11, 23
environmental footprints,   4
ethanol,   17

**F**

factories,   11, 13
fossil fuels,   9, 11, 14, 16, 17, 20,
    28

**G**

global warming,   11, 14
greenhouse gases,   14, 17, 30

**H**

human-powered travel,   6, 30
hybrid cars,   16

**M**

manufacturing vehicles,   10–13
mining,   12
mixed developments,   22
motorbikes,   7
multiple-occupancy lanes,   18

**N**

natural resources,   4
nonrenewable resources,   10

**P**

packaging,   13
petroleum oil,   10
pollution,   5, 9, 11, 14–15, 16,
    18, 20, 21, 25
population growth,   4, 20, 21
public transportation,   15, 18,
    20, 22, 23, 26, 29

**R**

rail travel,   7
recyclable vehicles,   12, 28
resources,   10, 12, 24, 28
reusing parts,   13
road congestion,   9, 20–22

**S**

scooters,   7
sharing rides,   18, 26
skateboarding,   6
streetcars,   18, 22

**T**

trains,   7, 18, 22, 26
transportation industry,   6–9
transportation system,   6, 8, 24
travel footprint,   5, 28–29

**V**

Volkswagen factory, Wolfsburg
    (Germany),   13

**W**

walking,   6, 7, 26, 27, 29
walking bus,   27
waste,   9, 11, 13
water,   13, 24